I0447032

BOATERS' INVESTMENT IN CLEAN WATER: A REVIEW OF THE CLEAN VESSEL ACT

A Report by the
Sport Fishing and
Boating Partnership
Council

1992-2007

Avalon Harbor, Santa Catalina Island, California

Table of Contents

Acknowledgements

This report was edited by Andrew Loftus and Doug Hobbs with assistance and contributions from a number of individuals. We would like to thank Brian Bohnsack (U.S. Fish and Wildlife Service Division of Wildlife and Sport Fish Restoration Programs) and the Service's Regional CVA Program Coordinators who provided technical support and advice on the findings and recommendations. In particular, Tony Faast, Susan MacMullin, Julie Morin, Scott White, Jerry Novotny, Al Ortiz and Al Havens provided personal guidance and material throughout the review.

The membership of the States Organization for Boating Access (SOBA) shared their time and expertise in a number of areas vital to the review. The Association of Marina Industries, BoatU.S., and Recreational Boating and Fishing Foundation provided access to their lists of marinas and boating members (BoatU.S.) for purposes of soliciting their input into this review.

CVA program coordinators from state agencies and Service personnel provided input into the review findings and material for case studies contained within this report, including Kevin Atkinson (California Department of Boating and Waterways), Wayne Shuyler and Janine Belleque (Oregon State Marine Board) Anne Smith (Virginia Department of Health), and Judson Spicer (U.S. Fish and Wildlife Service).

The U.S. Fish and Wildlife Service Division of Wildlife and Sport Fish Restoration Programs provided extensive logistical support and information that was needed to conduct a thorough evaluation of the program. Phil Million and Doug Hobbs, of the U.S. Fish and Wildlife Service Division of Conservation Partnerships provided coordination and financial support for the assembly and printing of the report. The review was conducted under the auspices of the Sport Fishing and Boating Partnership Council chaired by Dr. William W. Taylor.

Forward

Fifteen years after passage of the original legislation creating the Clean Vessel Act, the program can be deemed a success. By all indications, the program has fostered significant advances in achieving its goal of reducing the environmental impacts from recreational boaters. More than $134 million has been invested through the CVA program to achieve this goal and with recent amendments to the legislation authorizing this program, even more is expected in the next fifteen years.

Recognizing the benefits of a systematic evaluation of a program of this magnitude and maturity, the Director of the U.S. Fish and Wildlife Service (Service) requested that the Sport Fishing and Boating Partnership Council conduct an independent review to help "The Service expand awareness and use of the program and improve its delivery."

By all accounts, state and federal agencies as well as boaters and the boating community deem this program a success. As with any long running program, some changes will prepare the CVA program to build on this track record of success in the future. For example, the program and constituents would greatly benefit from improvements in accountability and measures of progress not only to make it more transparent to program partners and policy makers but also to help boaters pinpoint facilities more easily. Further, as a mature program, many of the facilities constructed with CVA funds are now showing their age. The top reason that boaters cited for failing to use a pumpout when one was needed was inoperable pumpout equipment. Public confidence and continued use of pumpouts by boaters relies on equipment being in working order when needed.

These recommendations and others are discussed and detailed in the pages that follow. In this report, the CVA Review Panel outlines a series of enhancements that we feel will make this a stronger program for America's boaters and the environment. Many of the recommendations are fine tuning procedures that are already in place, while others will require the commitment of the Service, states, and the boating community to effectively implement.

The boating community can be proud of the investments that have been made with their dollars through the Clean Vessel Act. The Sport Fishing and Boating Partnership Council stands ready to work with the Service, the states and the boating constituency to implement the recommendations outlined in this report and create a stronger, more vibrant CVA program that is ready to meet the challenges of the next fifteen years.

John Sprague
Clean Vessel Act Review Committee Chairman
Sport Fishing and Boating Partnership Council

Executive Summary

In September, 2006, U.S. Fish and Wildlife Service Director Dale Hall charged the Sport Fishing and Boating Partnership Council with conducting a comprehensive evaluation of the first 15 years of Congressional authorization of the Clean Vessel Act, focusing particularly on the following:

- Examination of the proposal submission and grant approval process with input from the Service's Regional and Washington Division of Wildlife and Sport Fish Restoration Programs staff, state coordinators, marina owners, and the Council's Review Panel;

- Identification of barriers to awareness and use of the program;

- Examination of the adequacy of the funding ratio between inland and coastal states;

- Recommendations on how to improve the administration of the CVA program to achieve maximum benefits for boating stakeholders and aquatic resources; and

- Clarification of the relationship between the CVA program and the Clean Marina Program.

To accomplish this, the Council established a CVA Review Panel. The panel worked with U.S. Fish and Wildlife Service Regional CVA program coordinators and Washington office program staff to develop a program of work and to collect information and insight into the workings of the CVA program. Constituents and representative groups including the States Organization for Boating Access, BoatU.S., and the Association of Marina Industries, were consulted in every phase of the review to gain an assessment of program effectiveness from the perspective of those most directly involved with at-the-waterfront implementation of the CVA Program.

Activities from 1992 to 2007 » pg. 15

Between 1993 and 2007, all eligible states/ territories except for Iowa, West Virginia, and Wyoming have requested, and have been awarded, funds from CVA, with more than $134 million invested through the CVA program. Although exact numbers of pumpout facilities (including pumpout boats) funded are unavailable, at least 2,700 pumpout and 1,800 dump station facilities were constructed in the first ten years of the program, according to a report from the Government Accountability Office.

Findings and Recommendations » pg. 16

By all indications, the CVA program partners feel that this program has done a good job with its intended purpose. Like any program, however, 14 years after its first implementation, adjustments can be made to improve its overall effectiveness, efficiency, and accountability. The findings and recommendations in this report are intended to highlight improvements. Wholesale changes in program direction are neither warranted nor desired.

The Application Process » pg. 16

Overall, the existing application process is working and is well accepted. However, the process can be improved through slight adjustments, and additional guidance. The Service should construct a single application process so that coastal states do not need to apply separately for inland and coastal projects. Additionally, standard guidance documents need to be developed for both project applicants (marinas) and states, as well as a standardized project application as an option for marinas to apply to their state for funding.

Barriers to Awareness and Use of the CVA Program » pg. 17

One of the authorized purposes of the CVA grant program is to educate recreational boaters about the need for pumpouts and inform them of the location of pumpout facilities. However, only 36% (362 of 1,011) of boaters recognized the CVA symbol; 51% (520 of 1,011) could not recall ever having seen this symbol. Despite this, 82% (818 out of 1,001) of BoatU.S. members indicated that, during the past five years, they had always used a pumpout when they needed one and one was available indicating a high rate of compliance. Most state agencies are not requesting CVA funds for education and outreach programs; only 17 states requested funds for such purposes between 2002 and 2006. More than one third (10 out of 27) of state administrators ranked education and outreach as their second highest priority (out of eight choices).

Boaters seem to be using pumpouts, but are unaware of the pumpout symbol, and states are either funding outreach programs from other sources of funds or not at all. Increasing boaters' use of pumpouts (the ultimate goal of the CVA program) and increasing the awareness of the symbol so that boaters associate it with a pumpout are both important objectives. Additionally, as part of their outreach, the Service and CVA partners should implement a system to allow boaters to report non-operating pumpouts in order to enhance user satisfaction with, and use of, CVA facilities.

Funding Ratio Between Inland and Coastal States » pg. 18

Following the intent of Congress, the scoring formula used by the Service is designed to provide an advantage to coastal state projects, but still allow some funding to be provided to each state applicant. Coastal funding averages 76% of the total funding available each year. While the CVA scoring criteria has served a useful purpose for the first fourteen years of the program, it should be updated to provide more utility under current day conditions. The Review Panel recommends increasing the maximum points possible for inland states to 45 while maintaining the coastal point cap at 50. Additionally, the scoring process should retain the point levels associated with "having a plan" and for "partnerships" but that for "sensitive areas" should be eliminated. Legislative changes should be considered to eliminate the criterion for "innovative." Criterion should be added to encourage states to implement an inspection program for ensuring that pumpouts installed with CVA funds are in operable order.

Fish and Wildlife Service Program Administration

General Administration » pg. 21

In general, the Review Panel found the Service's program administration to be acceptable. However, from discussions with state CVA coordinators and Service employees, there appear to be inconsistencies in what is considered eligible to be funded under the CVA program. Therefore, the Service should clearly define eligible activities under the CVA Program and ensure that all Service regions consistently apply this nationwide. Following the intent of the CVA legislation, the Service should encourage states to allow funding for all eligible activities, provided such activities are not prohibited through state statutes. Criterion should also be added to the scoring process that rewards states that use grant funds and close grants in a timely manner. For any state that wishes to create or update their CVA plan (inland as well as coastal), specific funding should be made available and the Service should assist the states in this development.

FLICKR / TOM HENTHORN SR.

Essex Yacht Club, Connecticut

Accomplishments Reporting » pg. 22

In collecting information for this review, the Review Panel had difficulty accessing comparable basic information regarding the accomplishments made through the program. The Service has not compiled the total pumpout stations constructed or pumpout boats purchased in recent years, and has not implemented a systematic way to collect this in a standard fashion. This lack of accomplishments information is problematic when trying to communicate the program success and needs. To rectify this, the Service, should develop a standard mechanism for accomplishments reporting purposes and amend the grant scoring criteria to award points to all states that provide the Service with all of the accomplishments information (both historical and current). Reporting will be further enhanced if the Service standardizes the financial categories for reporting and defines which items must be included in each category. Criterion should be added to support states that provide the Service with standardized accomplishments data and to states that fund maintenance funding (discussed later).

Maintenance of CVA-Funded Facilities » pg. 24

Maintenance of CVA-funded facilities is a significant issue. Sixty-four percent (21 of 33) of states responding to a questionnaire indicated that they do not provide operation and maintenance funds to subgrantees (marinas); yet boaters responding to the Review Panel's questionnaire indicated that inoperable pumpouts was the top reason that they did not use a pumpout when one was needed. This finding of inadequate maintenance is consistent with findings of a 2004 report of the Government Accountability Office. To rectify this will require combined efforts of government and marina operators. The Review Panel recommends that the Service specify seven years as a minimum period that a marina must maintain equipment and abide by the agreement (such as fees charged). This time period is measured from the last date that a marina received any CVA funds, and steps should be taken to ensure that this responsibility passes to the new owner of a facility when a marina is sold or transferred. To help fund maintenance needs, a special pool of funds for maintenance purposes should be established in each region from the recovered dollar allocations. Finally, the Service should create a scoring criterion that awards points for states that fund maintenance of CVA-funded facilities to encourage greater attention to this problem.

CVA Funding of Floating ("On-Water") Restrooms » pg. 26

For purposes of the CVA, a "floating restroom" is just that—a toilet facility on a floating structure such as a small barge, not connected to land or structures connected to the land. Such facilities are an innovative way to serve boaters who may not have on-board toilets or have boats with limited holding tank capacity, particularly in large inland reservoirs. These facilities currently cannot be connected to the shore in any way if they are funded with CVA—a definition intended to prevent the use of CVA funds for construction of land-based facilities. However, these restrictions may be impeding their construction near heavily-traveled waterways that would legitimately benefit boaters. The Service should develop guidelines to allow floating restrooms to be connected to the shoreline for purposes such as sewage disposal pipelines when on-shore facilities are impractical or impossible to provide. Floating restrooms of any type (connected to the shore or free standing) funded through CVA must have a clear purpose of totally serving boats from access on the water and be located off the shoreline.

Recovered Funds » pg. 27

CVA funds that are awarded to projects but are never used are currently returned to the Service regions or to the national office for use on CVA-related projects. There are no clear guidelines outlining how these funds are redistributed or clear reporting requirements that allow the determination of how much funding is redistributed by the regions through this mechanism. The amount of such funds that are redistributed by the regions (i.e., not returned to the Washington office) is unknown. The Review Panel recommends that 50% of recovered funds be allocated to the region for redistribution to states and 50% to the Washington office for CVA project funding. One half of each region's funds should be made available to marinas in that region for maintenance purposes. In addition to being used to fund currently-eligible CVA projects, national funds should be used to fund projects submitted by state CVA coordinators for the Clean Marina Program (if authorized by future legislation), life-cycle testing of pumpout equipment, annual CVA conferences, and other special projects directly related to the CVA.

Matching Funds » pg. 28

The basis for the CVA program is user pay, user benefit. However, fees paid by boaters and collected by federal agencies as part of the Federal Lands Recreation Enhancement Act are considered federal funds and therefore cannot be applied as a portion of the matching funds for CVA projects. This may be impeding some CVA projects in certain areas of the country. However, this issue is broader than either CVA or the Service, and should be addressed by a larger group. The Sport Fishing and Boating Partnership Council should take the initiative to fully investigate the issue of allowing user fees generated through this Act to be used as the required match for projects funded under the Federal Aid in Sport Fish Restoration Program.

Fees » pg. 28

The current standard fee allowed to be charged for pumpouts funded through CVA is $5. There is generally strong support from boaters and marina operators for maintaining pumpout fees at $5-$10 and strong support from administrators for a graduated pumpout fee. The Review Panel recommends that the $5 fee remain in effect for pumpouts less than 50 gallons. For pumpouts more than 50 gallons, marinas should have the option of charging $10. All efforts to allow pumpouts to be free should be supported.

Interaction Between the Clean Marina and CVA Programs » pg. 23

More than 650 marinas nationwide are now certified Clean Marinas and are found in 23 states (including the District of Columbia). The Clean Marina and the CVA programs share a common objective of reducing the environmental impacts of boating activities. However, Clean Marina has a broader application than CVA by promoting environmentally friendly marina operating practices. While there is generally strong support for the Clean Marina program, the program has not been authorized through federal legislation and CVA funds cannot be used for Clean Marina activities aside from the installation of pumpouts. The Review Panel recommends that the boating community, working in conjunction with federal agencies, and other Clean Marina partners, seek legislation that formally establishes this program and authorizes a new funding source that does not rely on the existing CVA funds.

Full findings and details of these recommendations are contained within the report.

What is the Clean Vessel Act Program?

In 1992, recognizing the need to provide adequate facilities for recreational boaters to dispose of waste from marine sanitation devices, the U.S. Congress passed, and President George H.W. Bush signed into law, the Clean Vessel Act of 1992. This Act is designed to "provide funds to States for the construction, renovation, operation, and maintenance of pumpout stations and waste reception facilities." Ultimately, the primary intent of the Act is to reduce or eliminate environmental impacts of recreational boaters.

The Clean Vessel Act program (CVA) is an extension of the exemplary "user pay, user benefit" structure established for fisheries and related projects under the Sport Fish Restoration Program of 1950. Through this mechanism, excise taxes paid by manufacturers of sportfishing equipment (and presumably passed on in part to recreational boaters and anglers) and fuel taxes attributable to recreational boating are used to support programs that invest back into projects supporting their activities. CVA funds are administered through the U.S. Fish and Wildlife Service to the states for on-the-ground implementation by marina facilities. Between 1993 and 2007, more than $134 million has been invested through CVA.

Legislative History[1]

The genesis for federal involvement in developing boating infrastructure lies with the National Recreational Boating Safety and Facilities Improvement Act of 1980, also known as the Biaggi Act for its Congressional sponsor, New York Congressman Mario Biaggi. That legislation directed that a portion of federal excise taxes paid by recreational boaters on gasoline used in powerboats be used to fund the

Recreational Boating Safety and Facilities Improvement Fund. This money, formerly retained in the Highway Trust Fund for road construction and improvement, could now be used by states for boating safety and facilities programs. Under the law, Congress still had to appropriate the money for this purpose but in subsequent years it appropriated funds only for the boating safety programs (administered by the U.S. Coast Guard), not the facilities improvement portion.

In July 1984, Congress incorporated the Biaggi Act into an amendment to the Federal Aid in Sport Fish Restoration Act of 1950, creating a new trust fund, which became popularly known as the Wallop-Breaux Trust Fund for its two sponsors, Wyoming Senator Malcolm Wallop and then-Congressman John Breaux of Louisiana. Formally named the Aquatic Resources Trust Fund, it divided the tax monies into two accounts, the Boat Safety Account and the Sport Fish Restoration Account. The 1984 Sport Fish Restoration Act mandated that states accepting these funds in the form of grants dedicate at least 10% to the development and maintenance of boating access sites such as launching ramps and related facilities for trailerable boats.

Enhancements to the Sport Fish Restoration Act, in 1988 and 1990, increased the funding available for boating safety and thus, the amount available for access facilities. Then, in 1992, Congress passed the Clean Vessel Act to provide funds to the states—from boaters' gasoline tax expenditures—to install and operate facilities to handle sewage from boats, including pump out stations and pumpout boats at public and private marinas. Congress also increased to 12½% (increased again to 15% in 1998) the

---

1 Consult Appendix A for a more detailed history.

amount of each state's allocations that had to be invested in boating access projects. Authorization for the Clean Vessel Act expired in 1998, and therefore no grants for pumpouts were provided to states in that year (funding resumed the following year after reauthorization).

Although the new funding for boating infrastructure stimulated tremendous improvements for boaters, most of the funds went to constructing and maintaining facilities that served primarily small, trailerable boats. Recognizing the need for facilities to serve larger vessels, the Sport Fishing and Boating Safety Act passed by Congress in 1998, created the Boating Infrastructure Grant Program for the purpose of constructing new berthing facilities or renovating outmoded facilities that would serve

"non-trailerable," transient recreational vessels, defined as boats 26 feet and longer. This Act also reauthorized the Clean Vessel Act portions of the program, and funding of pumpout projects resumed in 1999.

In 2005, the Safe, Accountable, Flexible, and Efficient Transportation Equity Act (SAFETEA) reauthorized the Wallop-Breaux Amendment to capture the entire 18.3 cent Federal fuel tax on motorboats and small engines being paid by anglers and boaters. This resulted in an annual funding boost of $100 million for the Sport Fish Restoration and Boating Trust Fund (formerly the Aquatic Resources Trust Fund). Significantly, this act also created a permanent appropriation for Boating Safety Grants similar to that in place for the Sport Fish Restoration grants.

MILESTONES IN BOATING ACCESS PROGRAMS

1980 National Recreational Boating Safety and Facilities Improvement Act of 1980 (Biaggi Act). Allows federal excise tax on gasoline that is used by boaters to be used for boating facilities.

1984 Federal Aid in Sport Fish Restoration Act amendments—incorporates the Biaggi Act, creates the Aquatic Resources Trust Fund, and mandates that each state spend at least 10% of its annual apportionment on development and maintenance of boating access facilities.

1988 Reauthorization of Boat Safety Account of the Aquatic Resources Trust Fund; authorizes survey of the number and type of recreational vessels and the fuel used by them.

1990 1990 federal budget reconciliation process allows 2.5 cents of the newly approved 5 cent federal gasoline excise tax to be deposited in Highway Trust Fund (1.08% passed through to Aquatic Resources Trust Fund, thereby increasing funding for SFR fishing and boating projects).

1992 Oceans Act of 1992 creates the Clean Vessel Act program that funds boat pumpout facilities and programs; increases the mandatory percentage of state allocations that must be invested into boating access programs to 12.5% by state or by region.

1998 Sport Fishing and Boating Safety Act of 1998—creates the Boating Infrastructure Grant program to improve facilities for large transient vessels; Mandates that states must spend 15% for boating access projects.; reauthorizes the Clean Vessel Act; increases the amount of fuel taxes paid by boaters that is transferred to the Aquatic Resources Trust Fund (although still short of full parity).

2005 Safe, Accountable, Flexible, and Efficient Transportation Equity Act (SAFETEA) reauthorized Wallop-Breaux and captured the entire 18.3 cent Federal fuel tax on motorboats and small engines being paid by anglers and boaters.

How Is the Program Structured?

The CVA Program is authorized under the Federal Aid in Sport Fish Restoration Act. The U.S. Fish and Wildlife Service administers all programs under this Act, with the exception of Recreational Boating Safety Program (which is administered by the U.S. Coast Guard) and the Louisiana Coastal Wetlands Program (which is administered by the U.S. Army Corps of Engineers). The programs administered by the Service include such boating-related activities as boating access projects, the Clean Vessel Act program, the Sport Fish Restoration Program, and the Boating Infrastructure Grant program (Figure 1).

The CVA program is administered through the U.S. Fish and Wildlife Service's Division of Wildlife and Sport Fish Programs. The mission this Division is to help conserve, develop, and enhance the Nation's fish and wildlife resources, and to protect the habitats of these resources for the continuing benefit of the American people. The Service's relationship with the states in cooperatively funding these programs dates back to creation of the Sport Fish Restoration Program in 1950 (and the earlier Pittman-Robertson Act passed in 1937 for wildlife restoration). With the addition of boating-related programs in 1984 through the Wallop-Breaux Amendments, the Service continued to develop strong partnerships with state agencies

Figure 1. Cycle of Funding in the Sport Fish Restoration Program

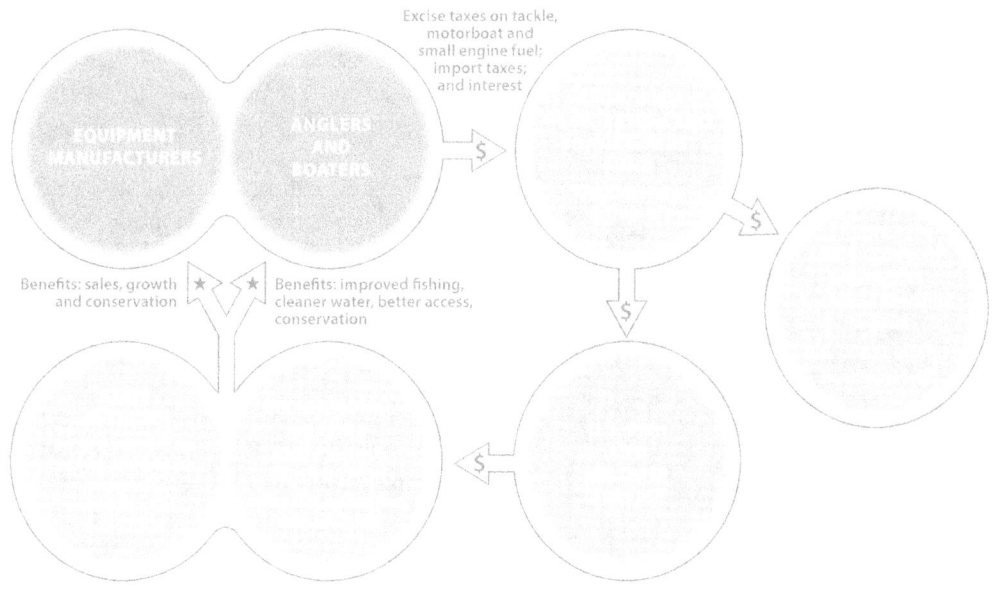

and with stakeholder groups. Thus, the Service was the obvious choice to administer the CVA Program in 1992 as well.

The Service receives funds for programs under Sport Fish Restoration, including the CVA Program, from excise and import duties on sport fishing equipment as well as gasoline taxes collected by the U.S. Treasury. The Service apportions these funds to the states and territories as specified by law. While the Service's Washington office provides overall program direction and coordination, the eight regional offices and the Washington Office provide direct interaction with the states and territories. In turn, each state/territory has designated staff to facilitate the transition of funds through each state's unique administrative structure to on-the-water implementation projects.

U.S. Fish and Wildlife Servicen Administration of the CVA

In accordance with the 2005 amendments to the Sport Fish Restoration Act, the CVA program receives 2% of all funds deposited into the Sport Fish Restoration and Boating Trust Fund. Each year, the Service issues a request for proposals to states, stating the amount of funding available for CVA grants. States, through their network of contacts and program partners unique to each state, notify marinas and other constituents of the funding opportunity.

Proposals from states are typically due to the Service by January 31st although this date may vary slightly. A state proposal generally contains requests for funding from multiple projects. The Service reviews and ranks the proposals using specific scoring criteria (published in the program rules, 50 CFR part 85), confers with other federal agency partners (Environmental Protection Agency, National Oceanic and Atmospheric Administration, and U.S. Coast Guard) and makes award decisions (Figure 2). Attempts are made to provide at least partial funding to most proposals.

The legislation creating CVA established a clear delineation between coastal and inland states, and the Service has implemented this distinction in several ways. In the current application process, coastal states that apply for both coastal and inland projects must submit a separate grant application for each. Further, through the scoring process (detailed later), coastal projects are provided with an advantage to ensure that a "coastal preference" for funding is maintained.

Figure 2. Clean Vessel Act Grant Cycle.

Step 1: The Service notifies the states and territories of the request for proposals (RFP) and the proposal deadline. RFP is posted onto Grants.gov.

Step 2: States and Territories prepare proposals. Typical timeframe will allow 60–90 days for the grant proposals to be submitted.

Step 3: The Service's Regional office personnel review proposals for completeness and request additional clarifications or material as needed. The Regional staff score final complete proposals, and forward on to the Service Washington office. (Approximately one month)

Step 4: The Service's Washington office conducts second review for completeness, scores proposals, makes preliminary funding recommendations, consults the Environmental Protection Agency, U.S. Coast Guard and National Oceanic and Atmospheric Agency for their review and recommendations. (Approximately two months)

Step 5: The Service's Washington office staff submits final funding recommendations to the Service Director. (Approximate timeframe 2–3 weeks) Director makes final funding determination and notifies the Service Directorate of decision. Directorate notifies Regions of the awards. Regions notify states and Territories of decision.

Step 6: States and Territories submit final documentation to the Service to obligate awards. States have two years to obligate funds or they are reverted. Regional office reviews final documentation to ensure substantiality of documents, assures NEPA compliance and other reviews (e.g., Section 7 Endangered Species). Regional office approves obligation of grant funds.

Step 7: State CVA grants are approved for a timeframe 1–4 years.

Step 8: Grants are closed. Final financial and accomplishment report are completed by the states and are due to the Service 90 days after the close of the grant.

Step 9: Funds remaining after the close of a grant (recovered funds) remain under the control of the Regional office and may either be returned to the overall funding allocation for the coming year or redistributed within the Region.

Grant Scoring Process

The state proposals submitted to the Service are scored on to the following criteria:

- Construct with a plan (coastal applications only)
- Partnerships
- Innovative
- Sensitive areas
- Low pumpout ratio
- Educational

The first three criteria are prescribed in legislation while the remainder are contained in Service regulations. As all of the coastal states have previously submitted their CVA plans to the Service, the current grant scoring criteria has a 50 point maximum for coastal applications and a 23 point maximum for inland applications. Under the formula developed by the Service, inland applications are at a 54% disadvantage in terms of money awarded. Currently, Coastal states can receive two awards in each grant cycle: one as a coastal state and one as an inland state. The maximum grant award has been limited to $1,000,000 or 10% of available funds (again, a state grant may be composed of several projects). This maximum is a policy established by the Service, not in law.

After proposals are scored by the Service regions and Washington office, they undergo review and comment by a multiagency federal review committee. Final decisions on funding are made by the Director of the Service. State agencies administer the grants to marinas in their state who conduct the on the ground implementation. Details of the scoring criteria and decision making process are found in Appendix B and are discussed further in the Review Findings and Recommendations.

SFBPC Review: Background and Process

In September, 2006, U.S. Fish and Wildlife Service Director Dale Hall charged the Sport Fishing and Boating Partnership Council (Council) to conduct a comprehensive evaluation of the first 15 years of Congressional authorization of the Clean Vessel Act grant program focusing particularly on the following:

■ **Examination** of the proposal submission and grant approval process with input from the Service's Regional and Washington Division of Wildlife and Sport Fish Restoration Programs staff, state coordinators, marina owners, and the council's Review Panel;

■ **Identification** of barriers to awareness and use of the program;

■ **Examination** of the adequacy of the funding ratio between inland and coastal states;

■ **Recommendations** on how to improve the administration of the CVA program to achieve maximum benefits for boating stakeholders and aquatic resources; and

■ **Clarification** of the relationship between the CVA program and the Clean Marina Program.

To accomplish this, the Council appointed a CVA Program Review Panel composed of representatives from the marina industry, state agencies, the Service, boating organizations, and the education/extension profession. This panel initially met with U.S. Fish and Wildlife Service Regional CVA coordinators in September 2006 to solicit input and develop a plan of work. Following this, the Review Panel met to compile the initial input, research specific issues (with the assistance of the Service's Washington office staff), and develop an outline of potential focus areas for the review.

CVA Review Panel

JOHN SPRAGUE, Review Panel Chairman, Marine Industries Association of Florida

MARK AMARAL, Association of Marina Industries

BRENDA CLARK, Land Management Office, Michigan State University

PETER DAVIDSON, Corpus Christi Municipal Marina

BROOKE FISHEL, National Marine Manufacturers Association

MIKE HOUGH, State Boating Administrator, Kentucky (Retired)

MARGARET PODLICH, Boat Owners Association of the U.S. (BoatU.S.)

ED POOLOS, SOBA CVA/BIG Committee Chair/TN Wildlife Resources Agency

Ex officio
RYCK LYDECKER, Chair SFBPC Boating Issues Committee, Boat Owners Association of the U.S. (BoatU.S.)

Project Staff

DOUG HOBBS, U.S. Fish and Wildlife Service/Sport Fishing and Boating Partnership Council

ANDREW J. LOFTUS, Loftus Consulting, Technical Assistance

BRIAN BOHNSACK, U.S. Fish and Wildlife Service

A key tool for obtaining input from a broad cross section of the boating community and CVA administrators at all levels was the use of questionnaires. All questionnaires were conducted under the auspices of private and/or nonprofit organizations with which the Review Panel members were affiliated using an on-line survey tool to facilitate expedient returns and analysis of the responses.

State CVA Coordinators. With the assistance of the States Organization for Boating Access (SOBA), emails were sent to coordinators of the CVA program in each of the state and territorial agencies that are eligible to receive CVA funding. Thirty-four responses were received (from 56 eligible agencies). Twenty-four (71%) of these came from agencies in coastal (as classified by the CVA program) states and ten (29%) from agencies in inland states (Appendix C).

Marina Operators. BoatU.S. and the Association of Marina Industries canvassed their marina operator members, directing them to an on-line questionnaire. The list of marinas was supplemented with the listing of marinas maintained by the Recreational Boating and Fishing Foundation. This afforded the Review Panel an assessment of program effectiveness from the perspective of those most directly involved with at-the-waterfront implementation of the CVA Program. More than 5,000 marine facilities were contacted, with 352 responding to the questionnaire (Appendix C).

Boaters. Using a quota-based sampling design, the 324,447 recipients of the BoatU.S. *E-Line* newsletter were solicited for their experiences, views and knowledge concerning pumpout facilities and the Clean Vessel Act. For logistical reasons, the number of responses collected was limited to the first 1,021 respondents. The geographic distribution of respondents is detailed in Appendix C. Informal monitoring of the results as they were submitted revealed little change in the responses to specific questions (in terms of percentages) after the initial 500 responses.

Activities From 1992 to 2007

Since the initial year of funding in 1993, all eligible states/territories except for Iowa, West Virginia, and Wyoming have requested and been awarded funds from CVA. More than $134 million has been awarded to states and territories through the Clean Vessel Act through 2007 (Table 1). Nearly $102 million of this has been invested into 33 coastal states/territories with the remaining $32.5 million being awarded to 44 states/territories for projects on inland waterways (see Appendix D for breakdown by jurisdiction).

Table 1. CVA Funding Awarded to States, Fiscal Year 1993–2007

	Inland	Coastal	TOTAL
FY93–94	$2,036,475	$9,690,369	$11,726,844
FY95	$1,236,200	$5,840,705	$7,076,905
FY96	$1,239,000	$8,161,000	$9,400,000
FY97	$1,940,000	$7,460,000	$9,400,000
FY98	CVA program not authorized		
FY99	$2,290,000	$7,110,000	$9,400,000
FY00	$2,238,337	$8,361,663	$10,600,000
FY01	$3,286,770	$6,647,164	$9,933,934
FY02	$3,944,882	$6,158,361	$10,103,243
FY03	$2,928,169	$7,071,831	$10,000,000
FY04	$3,985,849	$6,879,634	$10,865,483
FY05	$2,080,877	$8,168,088	$10,248,965
FY06	$2,332,868	$9,931,899	$12,264,767
FY07	$3,021,654	$10,234,872	$13,256,526
TOTAL	**$32,561,081**	**$101,715,586**	**$134,276,667**

More than $134 million paid by boaters has been invested through CVA.

Findings and Recommendations

By all indications, the program partners (the Service, state CVA administrators, and marinas), and users (boaters) feel that this program has done a good job with its intended purpose although some issues that need to be rectified have been identified. Fifty-seven percent (15 of 26) of state administrators responding to the questionnaire felt that the program focus should remain as it is currently. Like any program, however, 14 years after its first implementation, adjustments can be made to improve its overall effectiveness, efficiency, and accountability. The findings and recommendations in this report are intended to highlight those areas and suggest actions to make improvements to the program. Wholesale changes in program direction are neither warranted nor desired.

By all indications, agencies, marinas, and boaters are satisfied with the way that the CVA program has worked in the past, but some adjustments are necessary for the future.

The Application Process

Based on discussions with Service regional CVA coordinators and headquarters staff, combined with questionnaire responses from state program coordinators, the existing application process is generally well accepted. However, the process can be improved through slight adjustments, and additional guidance to states on grant specific issues. Such adjustments will improve the understanding and compliance with the requirements. The review process revealed that:

- Eighteen of thirty-two (56%) state administrators are satisfied with the federal grant cycle as it currently is structured (5 of 32, or 16%, had no opinion). Some suggestions were made to accommodate state fiscal years that commonly start July 1.

- Twenty-three of thirty-two (72%) state CVA coordinators responding to a questionnaire felt that the "dual funding application" (required when coastal states apply for both coastal and inland project s) should be replaced by a single application (83% of coastal states alone felt this way).

- Eleven of thirty-one (35%) state CVA coordinators responding to a questionnaire indicated that a standard application would help in their participation in CVA; 45% (14 of 31) felt that it would have no effect either way.

- Twenty-two of sixty-three (35%) marinas which did not have pumpouts installed cited as a reason that they were unfamiliar with the CVA program or did not know funding was available to them.

Based on these responses and evaluation of the current process, the Review Panel makes the following recommendations:

1. The current grant cycle (applications typically due in early January and awards announced in late spring) is acceptable. The Service should make every effort to maintain a standard application and decision making cycle.

2. The Service should construct a single application process so that coastal states do not need to apply separately for inland and coastal projects.

3. The Service should develop a standard guidance document and standardized project application as an option for subgrantees (marinas) to use to submit to their state program. This would assist facilities to work with their state coordinators for funding.

4. The Service, working in conjunction with the states and the boating community, should create a guidance document for the Clean Vessel Act that provides state administrators with all of the current policies and guidelines dealing with the CVA program.

Barriers to Awareness and Use of the CVA Program

One of the authorized purposes of the CVA grant program is to conduct "a program to educate recreational boaters about the problem of human body waste discharges from vessels and inform them of the location of pumpout stations and waste reception facilities." As a small part of enhancing the recognition of pumpout facilities, the CVA program has adopted a standardized symbol that also indicates the availability of a pumpout. Only 36% (362 of 1,011) of boaters recognized the CVA symbol; 51% (520 of 1,011) could not recall ever having seen this symbol.

However, 82% (818 out of 1,001) of BoatU.S. members indicated that, during the past five years, they had always used a pumpout when they needed one and one was available. If

Guidance documents should be developed to help states and individual marinas apply for funds

BoatU.S. members are representative of the general boating public (those owning boats large enough to require pumpout facilities), this seemingly high rate of compliance could indicate that boaters have received the message about using pumpouts. Of those boaters failing to use a pumpout at least once in the past five years, inoperable pumpouts were the number of reason cited.

Most state agencies are not requesting CVA funds for education and outreach programs. Between 2002 and 2006 (5 fiscal years), only 17 states had requested funds from the CVA program for education and outreach programs. These requests composed 14–18% of those states total request in any given year. Nine of those states had requested funding for outreach in four or five of those years (possibly indicating a sustained program) while 12 had only requested funds in one or two years. Thirty-seven percent (10 out of 27) of state administrators ranked education and outreach as their second highest priority (out of eight choices). Additionally, six of thirty (20%) state coordinators felt that the CVA program should emphasize public education and awareness to a greater degree than it currently does.

All of this information is challenging to interpret. Boaters seem to be using pumpouts, but are unaware of the pumpout symbol, and states are either funding outreach programs from other sources of funds or not at all. Increasing boaters' use of pumpouts (the ultimate goal of the CVA program) and increasing the awareness of the symbol so that boaters associate it with a pumpout (particularly valuable to boaters plying unfamiliar waters) are both important objectives.

Although the majority of boaters do not recognize the CVA symbol, use of pumpout facilities appears to be high.

RECOMMENDATIONS

5. The Service and states should enhance the visibility of the pumpout symbol, so that a larger number of boaters will be familiar with it and associate it with pumpout facilities. Efforts could include working with ongoing boating initiatives of the boating community such as "Grow Boating," National Marina Day, and programs

of the Recreational Boating and Fishing Foundation. States are encouraged to re-evaluate their need for, and effectiveness of, education and outreach programs. CVA program partners are encouraged to improve their connection to the national boating and marina press in partnership with state marine trade associations and national associations such as AMI.

6. As part of outreach programs (e.g., web site, hot line, etc.), the Service and CVA partners should implement a system to allow boaters to report non-operating pumpouts in order to enhance user satisfaction with, and use of, CVA facilities.

Funding Ratio Between Inland and Coastal States

Over the years of the program, coastal funding has ranged from 61% to 87% of the total funding available each year, averaging 76%. As described earlier, in accordance with the intent of the Clean Vessel Act, the scoring formula is designed to provide an advantage to coastal state projects, but still allow some funding to be provided to each state that applies. The federal CVA law states:

OUTREACH KEY TO NEW ENGLAND'S CVA PROGRAM

Constructing pumpout facilities is only one part of an effective state program. Outreach and education activities are instrumental to letting boaters know where facilities are located, how to operate the equipment, and the reasons to use them. New England states have tackled this challenge using new technologies as well as tried and true approaches.

In Connecticut, where all coastal waters are designated "No Discharge Areas," the number of pumpouts available has tripled, from about 30 to over 90. Pumpout boats now provide convenient service in many harbors. In addition, Connecticut's boater education efforts now include two interactive kiosks where questions and answers on boat sewage handling are displayed. Agency staff take the kiosks on the road to numerous boat shows each year.

Focus on Customer Convenience
One key to increasing pumpout use is to make the service convenient for boaters. Normally a boater calls the pumpout operators and makes an appointment. However, in Bristol, Rhode Island boaters can alert the pumpout boat by raising a bright orange pennant when service is required. Participating marinas or harbormasters make the pennants available free of charge. Using the CVA pennants eliminates the need to call by radio or telephone and leave long messages or try to explain the location and description of the boat in need of service. This has spread to other locations.

"Priority—In awarding grants under this subsection, the Secretary of the Interior shall give priority consideration to grant applications that:

(A) in coastal States, propose constructing and renovating pumpout stations and waste reception facilities in accordance with a coastal State's plan approved under section 5603(c);

(B) provide for public/private partnership efforts to develop and operate pumpout stations and waste receptions [sic] facilities; and

(C) propose innovative ways to increase the availability and use of pumpout stations and waste reception facilities."

CVA regulations add criteria for projects benefiting sensitive areas, low boater to pumpout ratios, and are educational. The maximum score under these criteria is 50 for coastal and 23 for inland states.

While the scoring criteria (Appendix B) has served a useful purpose for the first 14 years of the CVA program, the Review Panel finds that it should be updated to provide more utility under current conditions. While coastal waters remain important, many of the inland waters that could benefit from pumpout services are sources of drinking water and provide opportunities for contact-based public recreation such as swimming, fishing, etc. As such, it is important that these waters be provided with facilities authorized under CVA (including floating restrooms) wherever possible.

Additionally, state CVA coordinators did not indicate strong support for requiring all states to have a plan (note that under current law, only coastal states must have such a plan). Only nine of thirty-two (28%) indicated that all states should have a plan while 56% (18 of 32) indicated that this was not necessary.

Thirteen of thirty-two (41%) state administrators felt that the coastal scoring preference should be eliminated (9%, or three of 32, were undecided). Breaking this response into coastal and inland states, endorsement for eliminating the preference came from 39% of coastal states surveyed (31% undecided) and 44% of inland states (22% undecided).

The criterion for "sensitive areas" is not well defined in the regulations. The Review Panel feels that all near shore waters (where pumpouts are located) are sensitive and differentiating the "importance" of one area over another can be difficult. From a practical viewpoint, it is rare that any CVA proposal fails to garner these points, making the criterion, as it is currently applied, of little value for differentiating the merits of different proposals.

Likewise, the criterion for "innovative," as it is currently applied, provides little value in differentiating the merits of proposals. The initiation of the CVA program in the 1990s increased demand for pumpout equipment and in the early years of the program the number of manufacturers and equipment available increased, making the innovative criterion useful at that time. However, advances in pumpout technology, techniques, and placement scenarios have stabilized and few truly innovative pumpout scenarios are ever presented in proposals. In a practical sense, almost all proposals receive points for "innovative," again limiting the utility of this criterion for its intended purpose of differentiating proposals for funding purposes.

RECOMMENDATIONS

7. The Service should publish the funding formula that is used to determine the amount of money each state is awarded in each grant cycle to make the program much more transparent.

8. The scoring process should retain the point levels associated with "having a plan" and for "partnerships."

9. The scoring criteria should be eliminated for "sensitive areas"

10. Legislative changes should be considered to eliminate the criteria for "innovative."

11. Criteria should be added to encourage states to implement an inspection program to ensure that pumpouts installed with CVA funds are in working order.

12. In order to make inland states more competitive, the Service should increase the maximum points possible for inland states but still retain a coastal preference. One option is to increase the possible total points for inland states to 45 and maintain the coastal point cap at 50. Such change would make inland states slightly more competitive but still retain the advantage for coastal states.

Scoring criteria should be revamped and made more equitable for inland projects while still retaining the coastal preference.

PARTNERING TO PROTECT A JEWEL IN THE BLUE RIDGE

FLICKR / DUSTIN PLANK

Smith Mountain Lake is one of Virginia's most popular inland waters. Nestled in the Blue Ridge Mountains, this 20,000 acre reservoir provides water based recreation opportunities within a few hours drive of large metropolitan areas, including Richmond and Washington, DC as well as providing a source of drinking water for area residents.

To protect the water quality of this lake, the Virginia Department of Health (VDH), in cooperation with the Clean Vessel Act program, funds several programs to educate recreational boaters as to the proper disposal of vessel sewage.

Since 1997, student interns from Ferrum College have staffed demonstration projects, visiting area marinas every Friday, Saturday and Sunday between Memorial Day and Labor Day to distribute lists of pump-out stations and information on the proper disposal of vessel sewage. The students offer free pump-out service, as well, with mobile units and a pumpout boat and the results speak for themselves. The students pump more than 5,000 gallons of effluent each year. In addition, during the winter, spring and fall months, VDH staff distribute educational materials at boat shows across the state. Agency staff also operate a pump-out boat at festivals and regattas on an as-need basis.

Fish and Wildlife Service Program Administration

General Administration

In general, the Review Panel found the Service's program administration to be acceptable. The major area of needed improvement is national guidance on the list of activities eligible for funding and the disparate manner in which the CVA program is applied in this regard. In discussions with state CVA coordinators and Service employees, there are apparent inconsistencies from region to region in what is eligible to be funded under the CVA program. It is unclear if consistent guidance on eligible activities is being provided by each of the Service's regions to the states in each region. The Review Panel found that all states do not fund all eligible activities available under the CVA program (e.g., states not allowing maintenance funding for pumpout stations to marinas under the CVA Program).

The Service's program administration is adequate but it should ensure that the CVA program is consistently applied across all regions.

Additionally, the Clean Vessel Act only allows funding to coastal states for development of a pumpout plan. Although state CVA coordinators did not express strong support for mandating that each state develop such a plan, they did recognize the benefits to those states that had gone through the process.

RECOMMENDATIONS

13. Following the intent of the Clean Vessel Act, the Service should encourage states to allow funding for all eligible activities, provided such activities are not prohibited through state statutes.

14. The Service should clearly define eligible activities under the CVA Program and ensure that all Service regions apply this consistently and provide it in the guidance document.

15. The Service should develop a scoring criterion that rewards states that use grant funds and close grants in a timely manner. This would promote financial responsibility and would discourage states from delaying the collection of funds. The criterion should stipulate that points will be deducted based on the percentage of funds remaining uncollected after two years of being obligated to a state by the Service.

16. For any state that wishes to create or update their CVA plan, specific funding should be made available and the Service should assist the states in this development.

Accomplishments Reporting

In collecting information as part of this review, the Review Panel had difficulty accessing comparable basic information regarding the accomplishments made through the program. The Service has not compiled the total pumpout stations constructed/ boats purchased in recent years, with the most current information available from the 1990s. The Clean Vessel Act requires that each project location be identified and that lists identifying such locations be transmitted to the National Oceanic and Atmospheric Administration for inclusion on nautical charts:

> "(A) Lists of stations and facilities. The Secretary of the Interior shall transmit to the Under Secretary of Commerce for Oceans and Atmosphere each list of operational stations and facilities submitted by a State under subsection (b)(2), by not later than 30 days after the date of receipt of that list.
>
> (B) Completion of project. The Director of the United States Fish and Wildlife Service shall notify the Under Secretary of the location of each station or facility at which a construction or renovation project is completed by a State with amounts made available under the Act of August 9, 1950 (16 U.S.C. 777a et seq. [16 U.S.C. 777 et seq.]), as amended by this subtitle, by not later than 30 days after the date of notification by a State of the completion of the project."

It is unclear if or whether such reporting occurs on a routine basis, and there is no indication that a centralized database of such projects is being compiled for easy reference. Indeed, accurate program statistics (e.g., pumpouts constructed, pumpout boats purchased, etc.) and financial breakdowns (e.g., funds actually spent on operation and maintenance, salaries, etc.) for the overall program are not available.

Additionally, since a diversity of project types are eligible for funding under CVA (e.g., installation of new pumpouts, repair and maintenance of existing pumpouts, etc.), it is not always clear where and when new pumpout sites are actually being made available to boaters (versus simple maintenance of existing facilities). Complicating this is the lack of specific standardized financial reporting guidelines for expenditures made using CVA funds.

Programmatic and fiscal reporting mechanisms must be improved to aid communication about the program to the public and policy makers.

RECOMMENDATIONS

17. Within 12 months, the Service, with help from program partners, should develop a standard mechanism for accomplishments reporting purposes for each CVA grant. These templates should be structured so that the information listed below (at a minimum) is captured in a consistent way by the Service:

   - Locations of installed pumpout stations, pumpout boats, and floating restrooms;
   - Whether each grant was a replacement of an existing pumpout, maintenance of an existing pumpout, or new pumpout installation;
   - Breakdown of expenditures into specific categories; (installation, operations, maintenance, outreach, etc.);
   - Specific outreach materials created under each grant.

18. The Service should amend the grant scoring criteria to award points to all states (inland and coastal) that provide the Service with all of the information (both historical and current) identified above.

19. The Service, working with the states, should standardize the financial categories for reporting and define which items must be included in each category. The Federal form SF-424A currently required for many financial assistance applications from the Federal government contains most of the recommended categories. These categories could easily be carried over to the reporting phase of each project. Financial categories should, at a minimum, include:

   - personnel (whether contractual or employee)
   - fringe benefits
   - travel
   - equipment
   - supplies
   - construction costs
   - other costs, and
   - indirect costs

20. At a minimum, the Service should require standardized financial categories from *project applicants (marinas)* that can be used for financial tracking purposes that coincide with the minimum reporting elements described in subsequent recommendations.

USING CVA TO PROTECT DRINKING WATER

Clean and safe drinking water supplies are of paramount concern to people around the country. In many instances, CVA funds have been used to help protect these sources. The City of Salem, Oregon, with a population of 146,255 applied for and received a CVA grant to place a third floating restroom on Detroit Lake, specifically to protect the city's drinking water. The city has a drinking water intake that is approximately 37 river miles downstream of the lake. Although the city does not take water directly from the lake, it feels it is important to protect the quality of the water in the reservoir before it reaches the actual intake. Smith Mountain Lake, Virginia (See case study on page 20.) currently provides drinking water for residents of Bedford County and additional permits for additional domestic water withdrawal are under review. The number of registered boats in the surrounding counties, many of whom use Smith Mountain Lake, has steadily increased since 1997. To help protect the water quality, this lake was declared a "No Discharge Zone" and eight pumpout/dump stations were constructed around the lake using CVA funds with an additional seven constructed using other funding sources between 1997 and 2005. CVA funds are now used to maintain some of these stations and protect the water quality for all users of this popular waterway.

Maintenance of CVA-Funded Facilities

While construction of new pumpout facilities and pumpout boats is the critical first step in an effective CVA program, maintenance and operation of these facilities is often the greater long term challenge. Thus, individual states have been allowed leeway to develop working arrangements with their marina constituents for operation and maintenance. Some states allow marinas to apply for funds for operation and maintenance while others do not. Sixty-four percent (21 of 33) of states responding to a questionnaire indicated that they do not provide operation and maintenance funds to subgrantees (marinas); yet boaters responding to the Review Panel's questionnaire indicated that maintenance of pumpouts (e.g., pumpouts out of order) is the top reason that they did not use a pumpout when one was needed. An overwhelming number of boaters (67%, or 110 of 167) who had failed to use a pumpout at least once in the last five years indicated that "pumpout equipment was not in working order when I needed it" as the primary reason for their action.

Boaters cited "inoperable pumpout facilities" as the top reason for failing to use a pumpout when one was needed. Maintenance of CVA funded facilities must be improved.

The Federal Clean Water Act allows a state to petition EPA to declare portions of its waters as "No Discharge Zones" but only after the state certifies that pumpout stations are available in adequate numbers. A 2004 report[2] of the Government Accountability Office assessed the Environmental Protection Agency's "process for determining the adequacy of facilities to remove and treat sewage in proposed no-discharge zones" and on the "extent to which EPA and the states ensure that adequate facilities remain available" after designation of such zones. The findings are pertinent to the Review Panel's concerns regarding the maintenance of CVA funded pumpouts. The GAO reported noted:

> "EPA currently requires states to submit general estimates of need for facilities (known as pumpouts) in state applications for no-discharge zones, but other information that would support site-specific estimates is optional. As a result, EPA does not receive this information consistently. Moreover, EPA generally makes its determinations on adequacy without site visits to evaluate the facilities identified in the applications to ensure, for example, that they are accessible and functioning. GAO found no EPA and limited state oversight of pumpout facilities after no-discharge zones are established...Because the success of no-discharge zones depends in large measure on adequate facilities, GAO believes that EPA should assess the continued adequacy of these facilities, seeking additional authority, if needed, to require periodic recertification or reassessments."

---

2 United States General Accounting Office. 2004. Water quality program enhancements would better ensure adequacy of boat pumpout facilities in no-discharge zones. Report GAO-04-613, a Report to the Honorable Jim Saxton, House of Representatives, May 2004.

Further, the report noted that "...boaters have raised questions about the condition and availability of pumpout facilities in some no-discharge zones, generally those that encompass larger areas."

The findings of the GAO report coincide with the concerns that the CVA Review Panel heard from boaters regarding the maintenance of facilities. Given that maintenance of pumpout seems to be a reoccurring issue, the following recommendations are made to help rectify this situation:

RECOMMENDATIONS

21. The Service should specify how many years that a marina must maintain equipment and abide by the agreement (such as fees charged). The Review Panel suggests the following guidelines:

   a. Marinas receiving CVA funds must maintain the equipment, and keep it accessible to the public, for a minimum of seven years;

   b. At anytime during those seven years, marinas may apply for maintenance funds to replace/repair broken equipment. The seven year timeframe would then begin again (i.e., seven years measured from the last date that a marina received any CVA funds).

   c. The Service needs to ensure that the states enforce this responsibility when a marina is sold or transferred.

   d. A special "pool" of funds for maintenance purposes should be established from the "recovered" dollar allocations. Refer to the "Recovered Funds" section of this report for further detail.

22. The Service should establish regulations defining the items that are allowed to be included in "Operation and Maintenance" and other expenditure categories. These regulations should apply uniformly in all regions of the Service.

23. The Service should create a scoring criterion that awards points to states that fund maintenance of CVA-funded facilities.

AMERICA'S RIVERS BENEFIT FROM CVA

FLICKR / JJ SCHAD

Anywhere that boaters ply the waters in America, CVA funds can be used to help protect water quality. Take the Missouri River, for instance. Prior to 2003, a portion of this waterway near Bismarck, North Dakota suffered from a considerable amount of illegal dumping of waste overboard. A lack of pumpout facilities to service nearly 5,500 boats registered in the surrounding counties was a contributing factor. During the summer of 2003, CVA funds were used to construct a sanitary sewage pumpout facility with a floating dockside pumpout system at the Southport Marina near Bismarck North Dakota. The pumpout system supported approximately 300 boat slips and helped to reduce environmental contamination in both the Missouri River and the Heart River downstream. These facilities provide recreational boaters with access to a low cost sanitary means to dispose of their waste along this major inland waterway and protect the water quality in North Dakota and well downstream.

CVA Funding of Floating ("On-Water") Restrooms

For purposes of the CVA, a "floating restroom" is just that—a toilet facility on a floating structure such as a small barge, not connected to land or structures connected to the land. Such facilities are an innovative way to serve boaters who may not have on-board toilets or have boats with limited holding tank capacity, particularly in large inland reservoirs. Providing facilities such as these in areas that are convenient and accessible to boaters during their excursion (as opposed to the beginning or end of their trip where they may have access to land-based facilities) reduces disposal of waste from small on-board toilets or the incidence of boaters going to the bathroom directly into the water.

Under CVA guidelines, floating restrooms must be designed solely for boaters. This restrictive definition is intended to prevent the use of CVA funds for construction of facilities on land that may only marginally benefit boaters (other funding sources are available for these facilities). However, these restrictions on the definition of a floating restroom may be impeding their construction near heavily-traveled waterways that would legitimately benefit boaters. Forty-eight percent (15 of 31) of state administrators responding to a questionnaire support allowing floating restrooms to be connected to the shore (29%, or nine respondents, had no opinion). While the Review Panel strongly supports the intent behind the restrictions placed on the definition of floating restrooms, some minor adjustments should be made to accommodate facilities that legitimately serve boaters but may not meet the exact definition.

Floating restrooms constructed with CVA funds must serve recreational boaters exclusively.

FLOATING RESTROOMS: A POPULAR CVA INNOVATION

FLICKR / STEVEN KASSING

Tillamook Bay, Oregon

Floating restrooms are an innovative way to serve boaters where facilities are often most needed—on the water. California, for example, has more than 90 floating restrooms on nearly all its major inland lakes and reservoirs, removing 1,000,000 gallons of waste annually. Oregon has 22, located in coastal bays, reservoirs, rivers and lakes.

"When we first installed floating restrooms, public reaction was mixed," reported Janine Belleque of the Oregon State Marine Board. "Some people thought they were just an outhouse nailed onto a float. But as we educated boaters and word-of-mouth spread, they've proved popular, especially with families."

Floating restrooms are far from rustic. Aluminum framing, non-slip fiberglass decking, unsinkable floatation pontoons, large holding tanks and solar powered flush toilet systems give the units lifespans of 10 years or more.

"We often receive unsolicited comments from boaters about how these facilities improved their boating experience," noted Kevin Atkinson of the California Department of Boating and Waterways. "Thanks to CVA funding, California is able to meet increasing demands for the program, with the pay off of cleaner waterways and more enjoyable boating."

RECOMMENDATIONS

24. The Service should develop guidelines to allow floating restrooms to be connected to the shoreline for purposes such as sewage disposal pipelines when on-shore facilities are impractical or impossible to provide. Such regulations should not encourage the use of CVA funds for land-based facilities or for facilities intended to serve boats docked at marinas. Floating restrooms of any type (connected to the shore or free standing) must have a clear purpose of totally serving boats from the water and be located off the shoreline.

Recovered Funds

CVA funds that are awarded to projects but are never used are currently returned to the Service regions or to the national office for use on CVA-related projects. Regions may redistribute these funds to other projects in their region—either to the state that returned them or to another state—for CVA projects. This can be helpful to meet emergency requests (e.g., rebuilding hurricane-damaged facilities) or to meet small funding shortfalls in specific projects. There are no clear guidelines outlining how these funds are redistributed nor clear reporting requirements. Therefore the amount and application of funds redistributed by the regions through this mechanism could not be determined.

Table 2. Recovered funds returned to the Washington office

Fiscal Year	Amount
2002	$103,243
2003	0
2004	$865,483
2005	$493,965
2006	$1,510,826
2007	$988,855

** The amount of recovered funds redistributed by the regions (i.e., not returned to the Washington office) is unknown. Large fluctuations from year to year are likely due to accounting changes.

A portion of recovered funds should be dedicated to funding maintenance requests.

RECOMMENDATIONS

25. Recovered funds (currently allocated to Service regions) should be reallocated so that 50% is allocated to the region for redistribution to states and 50% to the Washington office for CVA project funding under the following guidelines:

    a. Regions must report the use of these funds using standardized reporting.

    b. Funds can only be used for CVA projects. A special "pool" of funds (consisting of at least 50% of recovered funds in each region) should be made available to marinas in that region for maintenance purposes, unless an exception is granted by the Washington office due to lack of demand from marinas for this purpose.

    c. Appropriate use of funds returned to the Washington office (in addition to currently-allowable activities) would include (but not be limited to) funding projects submitted by state CVA coordinators for the Clean Marina Program (if authorized by future legislation), lifecycle testing of pumpout equipment, annual CVA conferences, and other special projects directly related to the CVA.

26. Recovered Funds not used/reallocated by the regions within one fiscal year of being made available to them will return to the Washington office for dispersal as outlined above.

Matching Funds

As with other programs under the Sport Fish Restoration Act, the basis for the CVA program is user pay, user benefit. However, fees paid by boaters and collected by federal agencies (or in some cases, vendors operating facilities for federal agencies) as part of the Federal Lands Recreation Enhancement Act are considered federal funds and therefore cannot be applied as a portion of the matching funds for CVA projects. Anecdotal information suggests that this may be impeding some CVA projects in certain areas of the country from going forward and as a result it may leave boaters insufficient onshore pumpouts to dispose of their sewage ashore on these federally controlled waters. However, the Review Panel does not have the sufficient information to ascertain the extent of this problem. Further, this issue is much broader than the CVA program or the Service; it may be impeding other federally managed projects not covered under this Act. As such any solution will require participation from agencies in addition to the Service, as well as a broad array of constituent groups.

RECOMMENDATIONS

27. The Review Panel recommends that the Sport Fishing and Boating Partnership Council take the initiative to fully investigate the issue of allowing user fees generated from the Federal Lands Recreation Enhancement Act to be used as the required match for projects funded under the Federal Aid in Sport Fish Restoration Act.

COURTESY OF BOATU.S.

Fees

CVA program rules establish the maximum per vessel charge for pumpout services at $5 although a state may apply for a waiver to allow a higher fee in their state. Some marinas provide pumpout services at no cost as an amenity for slipholders or an incentive to attract transient boaters.

The standard allowable pumpout fee should remain at $5 for quantities less than 50 gallons. The allowable fee should be raised to $10 for all pumpouts greater than 50 gallons. Efforts should be encouraged to make pumpouts free.

Twenty-four percent (7 respondents) of state coordinators indicated that their state had asked for and received permission to deviate from this standard fee. There is generally strong support from boaters and marina operators for maintaining pumpout fees at $5–$10 and strong support from administrators for a graduated pumpout fee, as is reflected in the following table compiled from responses to the question:

Table 3. What do you feel is the appropriate amount to charge for a pumpout?

	Marina Operators	Boaters	CVA Coordinators
$0 (pumpouts should be free)	26%	49%	10%
$5.00	24%	31%	16%
$7.50 –$10	34%	9%	16%
$20.00 or more	6%	0%	0%
Priced according to size of boat or amount pumped out	10%	11%	45%

RECOMMENDATIONS

28. The $5 fee should remain in effect for pumpouts of less than 50 gallons. For pumpouts more than 50 gallons, marinas should have the option of charging $10 (regardless of the amount over) to help offset direct expenses (sewage disposal, water, etc.). The mechanism allowing states to apply for a waiver to these costs should remain in effect.

29. CVA partners should make every effort to provide pumpouts at no charge.

Interaction Between the Clean Marina and CVA Programs

According to the NOAA Office of Ocean and Coastal Resource Management, the Clean Marina Initiative "is a voluntary, incentive-based program promoted by NOAA and others that encourages marina operators and recreational boaters to protect coastal water quality by engaging in environmentally sound operating and maintenance procedures." The Clean Marina program has been extended to include inland as well as coastal waters. According to BoatU.S., more than 650 marinas nationwide are now certified Clean Marinas and are found in 23 states (including the District of Columbia). While these programs complement each other, and many certified Clean Marinas will include CVA-funded pumpout facilities, these two programs are not identical. Thus, the Clean Marina and the CVA programs share a common objective of reducing environmental impacts of boating activities on the nation's waterways. However, Clean Marina has a broader application than CVA. It promotes environmentally friendly marina operating practices, such as appropriate use and handling of chemicals at facilities, reducing oil and fuel spills in waters around marinas, and many others.

Antioch Marina, California

Clean Marina is a valuable program that should be authorized to receive federal funding.

Clean Marina is a voluntary program, and facilities are "certified" as Clean Marinas using criteria generally established by individual state programs. CVA is solely focused on reducing sewage discharge from boats. The two programs are often administered through different entities within a given state.

There is generally strong support for the Clean Marina programs, but the program has not been authorized through federal legislation. The use of CVA funds for certification/recertification of Clean Marinas is currently not allowed, but five of seven state agency administrators who currently have ongoing Clean Marina programs in their state support using CVA funds for recertification. While the Review Panel recognizes the value of the Clean Marina program and is interested in promoting its application, the program currently falls outside the purview of the CVA program.

RECOMMENDATIONS

30. The boating community, working in conjunction with the appropriate federal agencies, and other Clean Marina partners, should seek legislation to create and fund a nationwide Clean Marina Program. Given the commonalities in basic objectives between CVA and Clean Marinas, combined with the support of state administrators for developing a formal program and funding mechanism for the Clean Marina Program, the Review Panel feels that some resolution should be developed that provides funding authorization and a new funding source that does not rely on the existing CVA funds.

CVA PROTECTING ALASKA'S COASTAL WATERS

Juneau, Alaska's Aurora Harbor marina faced a dilemma common to many marinas around the country. Although pumpout equipment had been installed in years past, its location on the fuel dock meant that boats only used the service when re-fueling. Often, boaters who did not need fuel were either reluctant to occupy that space or did not want to wait for access to the pumpout.

Using a $100,000 CVA grant, Juneau installed a new system powered by a single pump, but providing five new connections along the harbor's main float, every 140 feet. Boats with assigned slips near the main float are able to pump out their holding tanks while in their slip. Other boaters, including transients, are able to temporarily moor in specially designated zones to service their holding tanks without blocking the fuel dock or other boats. This measure of convenience should result in more boaters properly disposing of their sewage, thereby reducing discharge of untreated sewage into Alaska's coastal waters.

Conclusion

Throughout the review process, the Review Panel encountered strong support and enthusiasm for the intent and accomplishments of the CVA program. Clearly, the program has served America's boaters well over the past 15 years.

Fifteen years after passage of the original legislation creating the Clean Vessel Act, the program can be deemed a success.

Looking ahead, several changes will help prepare this program for the future. In several sections of this document, the Review Panel has recommended areas of refinement in the scoring process used to determine the allocation of state grants.

The following table summarizes these changes:

Table 4. Refining the Scoring Criteria for Allocating Funds

| | RECOMMENDATION | |
Current Criterion	Coastal	Inland
Construct with a plan	Keep	N/A
Partnerships	Keep	Keep
Innovative	Seek legislative change to eliminate	Seek legislative change to eliminate
Sensitive areas	Eliminate	Eliminate
Low pumpout ratio	Keep	Keep
Educational	Keep	Keep
Proposed New Criterion		
Pumpout Inspection Program	Add	Add
Number of open grants	Subtract points for each grant open beyond 2 years	Subtract points for each grant open beyond 2 years
Reporting of accomplishments	Add	Add
State funds maintenance activities	Add	Add

N/A = currently not applicable.

One area of needed emphasis found by the Review Panel is improvements in accountability and measures of progress. While efforts were made in the early years of the program to track and document the installation of pumpout facilities and pumpout boats, the lack of a consistent reporting mechanism has hindered accurate assessment of CVA-funded facilities now available nationwide and their locations. Beyond the need for fundamental accountability and transparency, the inability to pinpoint pumpout locations may also hinder public awareness and use of such facilities.

Needed maintenance of the infrastructure created with CVA investments is an emerging issue that will become increasingly important as equipment becomes even older. The top reason that boaters cited for failing to use a pumpout when one was needed was inoperable pumpout equipment. Boaters who make extra efforts to reach pumpout facilities, only to find them unusable, may lose interest and forgo this extra effort when a pumpout is needed the next time. Maintenance of existing pumpouts must be addressed through incentives and enforcement of obligations associated with receiving CVA funds.

The basis for allocation of funding between coastal and inland projects appears to have served this program well in the early years. Minor adjustments to the funding formula would help to meet the growing needs for CVA projects in inland states while maintaining the competitive edge for coastal regions as intended in the original legislation. Adjusting the formula can also be a means to meet revised program objectives, such as the aforementioned need for attention to the maintenance of facilities.

Overall, the CVA program can be declared a success. This report does not delve deeply into the mechanics of implementing the recommendations; this function is left for the Service and program partners to address. The Sport Fishing and Boating Partnership Council is encouraged that the Service recognizes the value in making refinements to this program to meet the demands of the future and stands ready to work with the Service and all CVA program partners to help in meeting these challenges.

Haines Memorial State Park, Rhode Island

Appendices

Appendix A: Detailed Legislative History of the Clean Vessel Act[3]

The genesis for federal involvement in developing boating infrastructure lies with the National Recreational Boating Safety and Facilities Improvement Act of 1980, also known as the Biaggi Act. The legislation provided for a portion of federal excise tax receipts attributable to motorboat fuel use that formerly had been allocated to the Highway Trust Fund for road construction and improvement, to be transferred to the Recreational Boating Safety account. The Act authorized $10 million from this account for boating safety programs and $10 million for facilities construction and improvement. Although funds for facilities were authorized, Congress never appropriated money for this purpose.

In July 1984, through the leadership of Senator Malcolm Wallop and then Congressman John B. Breaux, the Biaggi Act was incorporated into an amendment to the Federal Aid in Sport Fish Restoration Act and was passed later that year as part of the Deficit Reduction Act of 1984. In recognition of Senator Wallop and Congressman Breaux, the Act took on their names and became known as the Wallop-Breaux Amendment. The major component established a new trust fund named the Aquatic Resources Trust Fund (the Wallop-Breaux Trust Fund) that was divided into two accounts: 1) the Boat Safety Account; and 2) the Sport Fish Restoration Account. Among other provisions, the Wallop-Breaux Amendment retained the collection of fuel tax revenues attributable to motorboats. The Amendment mandated that each state spend at least 10% of its annual apportionment on development and maintenance of boating access facilities. A broad range of access projects were eligible for funding, including construction of boat ramps and lifts, docking and marina facilities, breakwaters, fish cleaning stations, restrooms, and parking areas.

Provisions of the Wallop-Breaux Amendment required spending from the Boat Safety Account to undergo reauthorization after three years of enactment. Only the Sport Fish Restoration Account retained the "permanent appropriation" language of the original Sport Fish Restoration Act. Since motorboat fuel taxes collected in the Boat Safety Account that are in excess of the appropriated amount flow automatically into the Sport Fish Restoration Account, reauthorization affected the amount of money going to states for sport fishing and boating access projects. Unlike the Sport Fish Restoration Account, which is administered by the U.S. Fish and Wildlife Service, the Boat Safety Account is administered by the U.S. Coast Guard.

The reauthorization bill was introduced into the House Merchant Marine and Fisheries Committee in early 1988. In order to expedite passage, the language was later incorporated into the 1988 Coast Guard appropriation bill, which passed and became law (P.L. 100-448) in September 1988. The new law increased the spending authorization for the Boat Safety Account from $45 million to $60 million for fiscal years 1989 and 1990, then to $70 million for fiscal years 1991–1993.

---

3 Portions of this section are duplicated from: Radonski, G.C. 2000. History of the Federal Aid in Sportfish Restoration program. In: Rassam, G., A. Loftus, and B. Tyler (eds). Celebrating 50 years of the Sportfish Restoration program. Fisheries (25)7 (supplement).

Additionally, in order to verify the actual percentage of fuel taxes collected each year attributable to recreational motorboat usage, the 1988 amendments authorized the Secretary of Transportation and the Secretary of the Interior to jointly conduct a survey of 1) the number, size and primary uses of recreational vessels operating on the waters of the U.S.; and 2) the amount of types of fuel used by those vessels.

Two years later, the 1990 federal budget reconciliation process allowed for 2.5 cents of the newly approved 5 cents increase in federal fuel excise taxes to be deposited to the Highway Trust Fund. The Aquatic Resources Trust Fund, as in the past, received 1.08% of these new revenues.

In 1992, President George H. Bush signed the Oceans Act of 1992, which contained a number of environmental provisions. Title V of the Oceans Act was entitled the Clean Vessel Act, which included several modest changes to the Federal Aid in Sport Fish Restoration legislation. Among those changes were new distribution formulas to equitably distribute the additional motorboat fuel tax. The essential elements of this amendment created the Clean Vessel Program, a new cost-share program that made money available for construction, maintenance, and operation of facilities to handle sewage from boats. The new amendment made $5 million available for these purposes in FY 1993; $7.5 million in FY 1994 and 1995; and $10 million in FY 1996 and 1997. Additionally, an identical amount of spending authority was provided to enhance the state boat safety grants programs.

The amendments also increased the mandatory minimum percentage of state allocations that had to be invested in boating access and facilities projects from 10% to 12.5% for each state. Two changes were included to provide greater flexibility to states for their boating access and facilities projects. First, the act allowed an average state expenditure of 12.5%, measured across a region. The states were also provided five years in which to obligate their 12.5% boating access and facilities monies, again to provide flexibility to accommodate the imposition of the additional planning and permitting burden associated with the development of boating access.

The new funding available since 1985 for boating infrastructure improvements allowed tremendous improvements for boaters. Despite this, most of the funds were applied to constructing and maintaining facilities such as boat launching ramps that serviced primarily small, trailerable boats. Recognizing the need to address facilities for larger vessels, in 1998, the U.S. Congress passed the Sport Fishing and Boating Safety Act of 1998 (16 U.S.C.777g) as part of the Transportation Equity Act for the 21st Century. This Act provided $32 million over four years ($8 million per fiscal year for 2000-2003 for the sole purpose of installing, renovating and maintaining tie-up facilities for recreational boats 26 feet and longer and to produce and distribute information and educational materials about the program. Additionally, the 1998 amendments increased the mandated amount that states must spend to 15% from 12.5% for boating access and facility repair. Significantly, the 1998 amendments reauthorized the Clean Vessel Act (boat pumpout provisions) originally incorporated in 1992. Finally, the new amendments began to correct what many considered an inequity in the transfer of the motorboat fuel taxes. Prior to the amendments, the Aquatic Resources Trust Fund received only 11.5 cents of every 18.3 cents in federal gas tax per gallon paid by boaters and anglers. The 1998 amendments increased this to 13.0 cents on October 1, 2001 and 13.5 cents on October 1, 2003.

On August 10, 2005 President George W. Bush signed into law the Safe, Accountable, Flexible, and Efficient Transportation Equity Act: A Legacy for Users Act (SAFETEA–LU) which made some significant changes to the Sport Fish Restoration Program and reauthorized the Federal Aid in Sport Fish Restoration Act. The former Aquatic Resources Trust Fund was renamed the Sport Fish Restoration and Boating Trust Fund. With the merging of the Boat Safety Account into this account, provisions included a drawdown of funds in the Boat Safety Account over a five-year period, leading to the closing of this account in FY 2010. For the first time, all federal fuel taxes attributable to motorboats and small engines would be captured, resulting in an estimated increase in funding revenues from $472 million per year to approximately $570 million per year. The permanent appropriation language enjoyed by the Sport Fish Restoration Program was extended to Boating Safety Grants. Significantly, most programs in the new Trust Fund were funded on a percentage basis (as discussed earlier, some had been capped by a dollar basis) as follows:

■ Sport Fish Restoration Grants to States: 57%

■ Coastal Wetlands Act: 18.5%
  (includes COE and Service Grants)

■ USCG Recreational Boating Safety
  Program: 18.5%

■ National Outreach & Communications
  Program: 2%

■ Clean Vessel Act Grants: 2%

■ Boating Infrastructure Grants: 2%

■ Multistate Conservation Grants: $3 million

■ Fish and Wildlife Service Administration
  (Flat Fee adjusted annually for Consumer
  Price Index)

Appendix B: Grant Scoring Criteria and Process Used For Selecting State CVA Awards

Table 5. Point levels associated with each criterion in the CVA proposal review process

Criterion	Coastal	Inland
Construct with a plan	20	10
Partnerships	10	5
Innovative	5	2
Sensitive areas	5	2
Low pumpout ratio	5	2
Educational	5	2
Total Possible Points	*50*	*23*

Although the methodology for scoring grants has changed slightly over the years, the basic mechanism for determining the CVA program awards remains unchanged. The current version of that methodology has been applied since at least 1999, and is as follows.

1. Service Regional Offices use program criteria to score proposals submitted from within their region.

2. Proposals are rescored by the Service's Washington Office using the same criteria and, where differences occur, a consensus score is negotiated with the Regional Offices. The funding recommended by the Service for individual proposals that exceed 10% of funds available is reduced to a maximum of 10% of the funds available. In those states with both a coastal and inland component the recommended combined amount could exceed 10% since those states submit separate proposals for coastal and inland projects.

3. A selection panel with representatives from the Service, U.S. Coast Guard, National Oceanic and Atmospheric Administration, and Environmental Protection Agency review the project proposals and the Service scores.

4. The allowable proposal amounts that were calculated in Step 2 are multiplied by a factor computed by dividing the proposal's score by the top score (50) and converting to a percentage of the maximum (50 points). The product represents a weighted amount of the original proposal where the higher scored proposals receive a relatively higher amount than a lower scored proposal.

5. The proposals receiving $50,000 or less in the "Weighted" rankings are adjusted according to Step 7 below.

6. All proposals receiving less than $50,000 in the computation in Step 5 are awarded the amount of their proposal up to $50,000 in Step 6 to ensure all eligible states received a useful amount to initiate/continue a program.

7. Proposals funded in Step 6 are combined with the remaining proposals in the "Weighted" column and added into the total column.

8. All proposals in the Total column are prorated by multiplying the weighted amount calculated in Step 5 by a factor calculated by the total amount of funds available by the total amount of weighted requests (Total column). The results are sorted by score and these amounts become the awarded amounts.

Appendix C: Responses to the Questionnaires for the CVA Review

	State Coordinator	No. of Marinas	Marinas (%)	No. of Boaters	Boaters (%)
Alabama		5	1.40%	7	0.70%
Alaska		1	0.30%	2	0.20%
American Samoa		0	0.00%	0	0.00%
Arizona	X	2	0.60%	1	0.10%
Arkansas	X	1	0.30%	2	0.20%
California	X	32	9.10%	117	11.50%
Colorado		1	0.30%	1	0.10%
Connecticut	X	11	3.10%	45	4.40%
Delaware	X	1	0.30%	2	0.20%
Florida	X	42	11.90%	129	12.60%
Georgia	X	6	1.70%	16	1.60%
Guam		0	0.00%	0	0.00%
Hawaii		0	0.00%	0	0.00
Idaho		2	0.60%	1	0.10%
Illinois	X	10	2.80%	16	1.60%
Indiana	X	3	0.90%	5	0.50%
Iowa		0	0.00%	3	0.30%
Kansas		1	0.30%	2	0.20%
Kentucky	X	5	1.40%	10	1.00%
Louisiana	X	0	0.00%	5	0.50%
Maine		4	1.10%	8	0.80%
Maryland	X	22	6.30%	134	13.10%
Massachusetts	X	13	3.70%	66	6.50%
Michigan	X	14	4.00%	35	3.40%
Minnesota		7	2.00%	10	1.00%
Mississippi		1	0.30%	5	0.50%
Missouri		6	1.70%	7	0.70%
Montana	X	0	0.00%	0	0.00%
Nebraska	X	0	0.00%	0	0.00%
Nevada		1	0.30%	3	0.30%
New Hampshire	X	1	0.30%	1	0.10%
New Jersey		11	3.10%	51	5.00%
New Mexico	X	1	0.30%	1	0.10%
New York	X	21	6.00%	80	7.80%
North Carolina	X	11	3.10%	26	2.60%
North Dakota	X	0	0.00%	0	0.00%
Northern Marianas		0	0.00%	0	0.00%
Ohio	X	10	2.80%	20	2.00%
Oklahoma		3	0.90%	2	0.20%
Oregon	X	6	1.70%	13	1.30%
Pennsylvania	X	2	0.60%	5	0.50%
Puerto Rico		0	0.00%	0	0.00%
Rhode Island	X	2	0.60%	9	0.90%
South Carolina	X	29	8.20%	18	1.80%
South Dakota		1	0.30%	0	0.00%
Tennessee	X	5	1.40%	15	1.50%
Texas	X	9	2.60%	30	2.90%
Utah	X	0	0.00%	1	0.10%
Vermont		2	0.60%	3	0.30%
Virgin Islands		1	0.30%	0	0.00%
Virginia	X	22	6.30%	36	3.50%
Washington	X	15	4.30%	57	5.60%
Washington DC		3	0.90%	7	0.70%
West Virginia		1	0.30%	1	0.10%
Wisconsin	X	5	1.40%	13	1.30%
Wyoming	X	0	0.00%	0	0.00%
Total Responses	**34**	**352**		**1021**	

Appendix D: Summary of CVA Awards by State, 1993–2007

Coastal

State	Type	Total Requested From Program	Total Awarded From Program
Alabama Coastal	C	$1,417,099	$1,423,929
California Coastal	C	$15,491,350	$10,977,269
Connecticut Coastal	C	$8,432,929	$7,979,729
Delaware Coastal	C	$440,700	$385,300
Florida Coastal	C	$41,714,312	$12,619,190
Georgia Coastal	C	$344,954	$223,954
Hawaii	C	$3,250,813	$1,623,000
Illinois Coastal	C	$300,794	$248,096
Indiana Coastal	C	$986,117	$558,856
Louisiana Coastal	C	$1,568,882	$1,293,453
Maine Coastal	C	$2,595,147	$2,527,397
Maryland Coastal	C	$11,323,595	$7,854,989
Massachusetts Coastal	C	$13,679,039	$10,914,066
Michigan Coastal	C	$2,902,000	$1,645,100
Minnesota Coastal	C	$203,333	$156,000
Mississippi Coastal	C	$633,750	$494,684
New Hampshire Coastal	C	$685,638	$655,638
New Jersey Coastal	C	$10,867,080	$5,813,104
New York Coastal	C	$10,612,634	$5,969,901
North Carolina Coastal	C	$1,001,500	$785,750
Ohio Coastal	C	$1,965,025	$1,930,025
Oregon Coastal	C	$4,051,018	$3,913,108
Pennsylvania Coastal	C	$548,929	$444,351
Rhode Island Coastal	C	$1,485,591	$1,305,990
South Carolina Coastal	C	$5,155,108	$4,351,943
Texas Coastal	C	$2,176,351	$1,981,806
Virginia Coastal	C	$4,162,050	$3,739,888
Washington Coastal	C	$9,240,500	$7,916,100
Wisconsin Coastal	C	$1,035,970	$679,970
Guam	C	$150,000	$107,000
Virgin Islands	C	$440,000	$264,000
Northern Mariana	C	$60,000	$60,000
Puerto Rico	C	$1,594,704	$872,000
Total Coastal		*$160,516,912*	*$101,715,586*

Inland

State	Type	Total Requested From Program	Total Awarded From Program
American Samoa	I	$65,000	$50,000
Alabama Inland	I	$2,197,822	$1,207,233
Alaska	I	$904,300	$766,800
Arizona	I	$630,816	$306,763
Arkansas	I	$697,757	$585,824
California Inland	I	$10,686,600	$4,987,985
Colorado	I	$288,101	$207,181
Connecticut Inland	I	$147,364	$147,364
Florida Inland	I	$8,701,876	$4,432,217
Georgia Inland	I	$225,794	$130,794
Idaho	I	$611,904	$373,369
Illinois Inland	I	$316,000	$278,000
Indiana Inland	I	$1,075,492	$743,327
Iowa	I	$0	$0
Kansas	I	$31,875	$31,875
Kentucky	I	$1,378,885	$882,892
Louisiana Inland	I	$493,040	$288,200
Maine Inland	I	$19,301	$19,301
Maryland Inland	I	$0	$0
Massachusetts Inland	I	$78,000	$60,000
Michigan Inland	I	$0	$0
Minnesota Inland	I	$419,206	$248,270
Mississippi Inland	I	$769,785	$323,246
Missouri	I	$467,720	$410,720
Montana	I	$97,850	$19,300
Nebraska	I	$360,000	$118,500
Nevada	I	$355,952	$175,202
New Hampshire Inland	I	$414,955	$341,655
New Jersey Inland	I	$222,000	$73,000
New Mexico	I	$120,000	$90,000
New York Inland	I	$5,163,197	$1,602,233
North Carolina Inland	I	$352,500	$204,500
North Dakota	I	$17,025	$17,025
Ohio Inland	I	$515,269	$465,375
Oklahoma	I	$641,934	$402,754
Oregon Inland	I	$7,045,746	$4,230,155
Pennsylvania Inland	I	$259,666	$206,911
Rhode Island Inland	I	$0	$0
South Carolina Inland	I	$2,519,796	$1,127,089
South Dakota	I	$74,687	$64,687
Tennessee	I	$6,426,369	$3,243,569
Texas Inland	I	$2,128,040	$1,037,388
Utah	I	$1,757,645	$722,240
Vermont	I	$74,260	$52,402
Virginia Inland	I	$680,250	$452,685
Washington Inland	I	$1,825,500	$1,187,150
West Virginia	I	$0	$0
Wisconsin Inland	I	$96,725	$91,500
Wyoming	I	$0	$0
Washington, DC	I	$227,500	$154,400
Total Inland Requests		*$61,583,504*	*$32,561,081*
Total Coastal and Inland		**$444,200,832**	**$134,276,667**

Appendix E: Director's Letter Commissioning the CVA Review

In Reply Refer To:
FWS/AWSR/FA: 027124

SEP 14 2006

Dr. William W. Taylor
Chairman, Sport Fishing and Boating
  Partnership Council
Department of Fisheries and Wildlife
Michigan State University
7 Natural Resources Building
East Lansing, Michigan 48824-1222

Dear Dr. Taylor:

The Sport Fishing and Boating Partnership Council has been an indispensable source of advice for the U.S. Fish and Wildlife Service (Service) and the Department of the Interior. The council's recommendation on how the Service could improve delivery of the Boating Infrastructure Tier II Grant program (BIG) is one such example. The council's contributions will help us manage the program in a more efficient and focused manner.

Building on this record of success, we are asking the council to lead a review of the Service's Clean Vessel Act (CVA) grant program. This important program has provided funding for sanitary pump-out infrastructure that prevents the despoilment of our Nation's aquatic resources. However, the program has never been systematically reviewed over its 16-year existence. A review such as we are proposing would help the Service expand awareness and use of the program and improve its delivery. Potential items for inclusion in such a review include:

- examination of the proposal submission and grant approval processes with input from the Service's Regional and Washington Federal Assistance staff, State coordinators, marina owners, and the council's review team;
- identification of barriers to awareness and use of the program;
- examination of the adequacy of the funding ratio between inland and coastal States;
- recommendations on how to improve the administration of the CVA program to achieve maximum benefits for boating stakeholders and aquatic resources; and
- clarification of the relationship between the CVA program and the Clean Marina program.

If you agree to undertake the project, we ask that you coordinate your review and actively participate in the Service's policy and regulatory review of the CVA program that will begin later this year. It will include the development of pre-award Service Manual chapters on the CVA and BIG programs and the review and revision of regulations at 50 CFR, parts 85 and 86. We are hopeful that you will be able to share at least the preliminary results of your work with us by the summer of 2007.

Thank you for your interest in the CVA Grant Program. To discuss this request further, please contact Assistant Director Rowan Gould of Wildlife and Sport Fish Restoration at 202-208-1050 or Jim Greer, Chief of the Division of Federal Assistance at 703-358-2156.

Sincerely,

H. Dale Hall

DIRECTOR

www.ingramcontent.com/pod-product-compliance
Lightning Source LLC
Chambersburg PA
CBHW082200290526
45794CB00008B/3369